CHINA

Old Ways Meet New

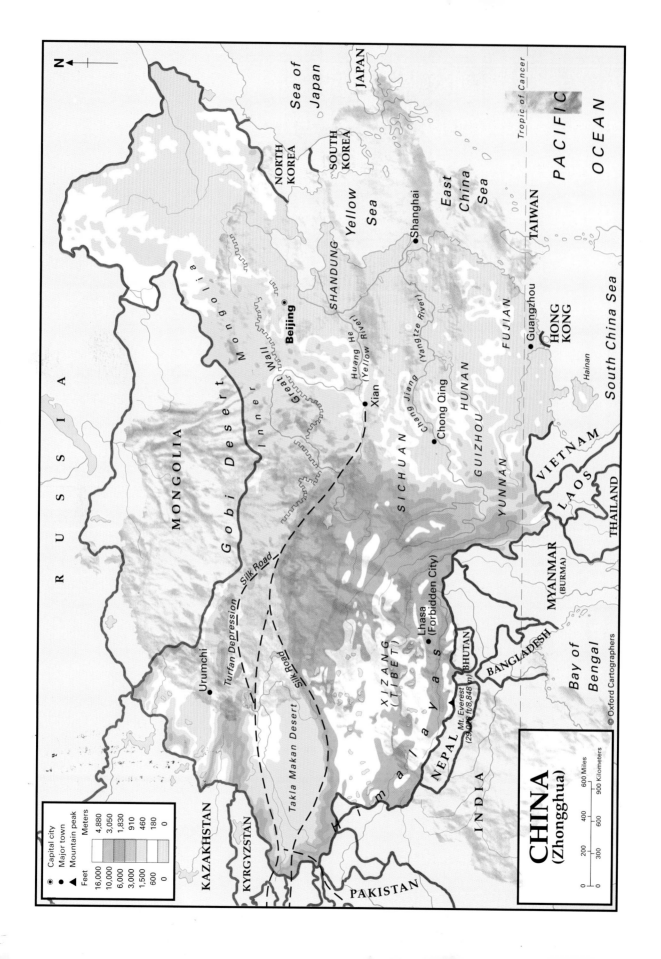

N

Sea of
Japan

JAPAN

NORTH
KOREA

SOUTH
KOREA

Yellow
Sea

East
China
Sea

Tropic of Cancer

PACIFIC

OCEAN

R U S S I A

M O N G O L I A

Mongolia

Gobi Desert

Inner

Great Wall

Beijing

SHANDUNG

Huang He
(Yellow River)

Shanghai

TAIWAN

Xian

Chang Jiang (Yangtze River)

Chong Qing

HUNAN

FUJIAN

Guangzhou

HONG
KONG

GUIZHOU

Hainan

South China Sea

Silk Road

Urumchi

Tufan Depression

Silk Road

Takla Makan Desert

SICHUAN

YUNNAN

VIETNAM

LAOS

THAILAND

MYANMAR
(BURMA)

X I Z A N G
(T I B E T)

Lhasa
(Forbidden City)

BHUTAN

BANGLADESH

Bay of
Bengal

H i m a l a y a s

NEPAL

Mt. Everest
(29,028 ft/8,848 m)

I N D I A

KAZAKHSTAN

KYRGYZSTAN

PAKISTAN

© Oxford Cartographers

Capital city
Major town
Mountain peak

Feet   Meters
16,000   4,880
10,000   3,050
6,000   1,830
3,000   910
1,500   460
600   180
0   0

CHINA
(Zhongghua)

600 Miles
900 Kilometers
0   200   400   600
0   300   600

EXPLORING CULTURES OF THE WORLD

CHINA

Old Ways Meet New

Deborah Kent

BENCHMARK BOOKS

MARSHALL CAVENDISH

NEW YORK

*With thanks to Anita Siu of the
Department of Asian Art, The Metropolitan Museum of Art, New York City,
for her expert reading of the manuscript.*

Benchmark Books
Marshall Cavendish Corporation
99 White Plains Road
Tarrytown, New York 10591-9001

© Marshall Cavendish Corporation 1996

Library of Congress Cataloging-in-Publication Data

Kent, Deborah.
    China : old ways meet new/by Deborah Kent
        p.   cm. — (Exploring cultures of the world)
    Includes bibliographical references and index.
    ISBN 0-7614-0202-0 (library binding)
    1. China—Civilization—Juvenile literature. 2. China.   I. Title. II. Series.
  DS721.K45   1996
  951—dc20   95-44126
SUMMARY: Discusses the geography, history, people, culture, customs, and the arts of China.

Printed and bound in the U.S.A.
Book design by Carol Matsuyama
Photo research by Sandy Jones

Photo Credits

Front cover: courtesy of FPG International/Travelpix; back cover and page 44: courtesy of FPG International/Antoinette Jongen; title page and pages 13, 34: courtesy of Tony Stone Worldwide/Jean-Marc Truchet; page 6: China Stock/Ru Suichu; page 9: Tom Stack & Associates/Manfred Gottschalk; page 10: The Image Bank/Anne Rippy; page 11: ©Catherine Gehm; page 14: The Image Bank/Guido Alberto Rossi; page 16: China Stock/Zhao Liye; page 18: FPG International/Travelpix; pages 20 *(top)*, 29: Tony Stone Worldwide/Alain Le Garsmeur; page 20 *(bottom):* ©Carl Purcell; pages 23, 45: Unicorn Stock Photos/Goe Sohm; page 24: ©Mary Altier; pages 25, 52: ©Wolfgang Kaehler; page 27: Tony Stone Worldwide/Julian Engelsman; page 30: The Image Bank/Grant V. Faint; pages 33, 47: FPG International/Ann & Myron Sutton; pages 36, 48: FPG International/Ken Ross; page 37: China Stock/Liu Qijun; page 39: FPG International/Dave Bartruff; page 41: ©Michele Burgess; page 42: China Stock/Dennis Cox; page 49: China Stock/Gin Yaowen; page 50: Tony Stone Worldwide/Sylvain Grandadam; page 54: ©Suzanne L. Murphy; page 55: FPG International/Jean Kugler; page 56: FPG International/Dennis Cox

Poetry, page 53: From *Chinese Literature: An Anthology from the Earliest Times to the Present Day,* edited by William McNaughton. Rutland, Vermont, and Tokyo: Charles E. Tuttle, 1974.

Contents

宋徽宗四年 允迪路公
奉命使之島麗遇颶
危蕩皆二神女坐于
檣上風即此浹
命于朝賜額至
廟

Mazu, Queen of Heaven, protects sailors and fishermen.

1

GEOGRAPHY AND HISTORY

The Ancient Land of China

Mazu, the Queen of Heaven

About a thousand years ago, a little girl from Fujian (foo-gee-EN) Province sat with her mother. Suddenly her body went stiff, and she did not answer when her mother called to her. No one knew that the little girl, Mazu, had strange, supernatural powers. She had seen her two older brothers caught in a terrible storm miles away at sea. As her mother wept and shook her, Mazu's spirit flew over the water to the wildly tossing boat. She gathered her brothers into her arms and carried them safely to shore. Over the years that followed, she used her remarkable powers to rescue many drowning sailors and fishermen.

According to the story, Mazu never married, but spent her life with her family. Two companions aided her in her rescue work, the brothers Thousand-Mile Eye and Fair-Wind Ear. The brothers had special powers of their own. One could see what was happening far away, while the other could hear storms from an impossible distance.

Many Chinese scholars believe that Mazu really existed. They think she lived around A.D. 1000. But almost nothing is known about her actual life. In southern China she is worshiped as a goddess, the Queen of Heaven. Travelers pray to her, asking for a safe journey. On Mazu's birthday the people of China's southern coast celebrate with displays of glorious fireworks. As flaming rockets light the sky, they think of the little girl who carried her brothers home in her arms.

The Land of Two Great Rivers

Sweating men stand ankle deep in water, urging a stubborn pair of oxen to drag a plow. The men are planting rice, the crop that sustains millions of Chinese people. To many Americans and Europeans (Westerners, as the Chinese call them), this scene represents all of China.

Most of China's flooded rice fields, or paddies, lie along the great Yangtze, or Chang Jiang (Long River), and its sprawling tributaries. The Chang Jiang (chahng gee-AHNG) rises in the mountains of southwestern China, near Tibet. It flows for about 3,900 miles (6,275 kilometers) eastward across the country to the East China Sea. The swift upper river, nearest to the source, carves its way through steep, scenic gorges and canyons. Further east, as the land levels into open plains, the river grows broad and sluggish. Here, along its eastern course, the Chang Jiang waters China's famous fields of rice. But the Chang Jiang rice paddies are only one part of the vast and varied land of China.

Just as the Chang Jiang is important to southern China, the Huang He, or Yellow River, has molded the northern part of the country. The Huang He (hwahng huh) earned its name because of the thick yellow dust that tints its waters. The river has a sinister nickname as well. It is often referred to as China's Sorrow. During heavy summer rains, the Huang He often

Animals are still used to till the fields in rural China.

overflows, causing deadly floods. Along its eastern course, it is contained between high man-made walls, or levees. In places the riverbed is so thick with yellow silt that the Huang He actually flows ten or twelve feet above the surrounding land. Only the levees keep the waters from breaking loose and engulfing the countryside. The cool climate of northern China is too harsh for rice growing. Instead, the people of the north raise other grains, especially wheat and millet.

The People's Republic of China, the land shaped by the Chang Jiang and Huang He Rivers, lies on the continent of Asia. To the north spread Russia (the former Soviet Union), Outer Mongolia, and North Korea. China's east and southeast coasts are lapped by three bodies of water: the Yellow Sea, the East China Sea, and the South China Sea—all connected to the Pacific Ocean. China's neighbors to the south are Vietnam, Laos, Myanmar (Burma), India, Bhutan, and Nepal. To the west, China is bordered by Pakistan and Afghanistan.

China's coast is dotted with some five thousand islands. The largest of these is Hainan (hi-NAHN), in the South China Sea. The island of Hong Kong, long under British rule, will be returned to China in 1997. The island of Taiwan (tie-WAHN), also known as the Republic of China, is an independent country.

In area, China is the third largest nation on earth. Only Russia and Canada possess more land. About one-third of China consists of rugged mountain ranges. The most spectacular of these mountains are the snow-capped Himalayas of Xizang (shee-ZAHNG), the Chinese name for Tibet. The

The sails of a Chinese junk stand in striking contrast to Hong Kong's high-rise towers.

Himalaya region is sometimes called "the roof of the world" because it contains the highest peaks on earth.

China also has some of the world's most hostile deserts. The largest of these are the Takla Makan and the Gobi Desert of Inner Mongolia. The Turfan Depression near the city of Urumchi is a desolate moonscape of shifting sand dunes 505 feet (154 meters) below sea level. The temperature in the Turfan Depression can soar to a pitiless 158°F (52°C)—so hot that one could actually fry an egg on the rocks.

From the towering Himalayas the land descends through lower mountain ranges, plateaus, desert basins, and hills. At last the hills yield to a level plain that extends to the coast. Only about 15 percent of China's land is useful for farming. Most of this arable land lies along the rivers on the eastern plains.

At one time nearly half of China was covered with forests. Over the centuries most of the forests have been cleared. Today about 8 percent of China's land remains wooded, mostly in the thinly populated western region. China's forests are home to leopards, bears, wolves, foxes, several species of monkeys, and the endangered giant panda.

In the Stone Forest of southwestern China, strange rock formations stand like densely planted trees.

The Mandate of Heaven

When Chinese people speak of events in their nation's past, they seldom refer to a particular century. Instead they say, for example, "This story takes place back in the Tang Dynasty. . . ." For more than four thousand years, China was controlled by a number of dynasties. A dynasty is a series of rulers who belong to the same family and rule for several generations. Each dynasty was unique, but in many ways they were all alike. Each one collected taxes, waged wars, and gained and lost territory.

During the early dynasties, most of China was divided into small city-states that were constantly at war. Then, in 221 B.C., a powerful warrior named Qin Shi Huangdi (CHIN sure hwang-DEE) united much of the land that is northern China today. The Qin Emperor, as he is called, claimed that he ruled with "the mandate of heaven." Each emperor that followed insisted that he ruled by heaven's special orders, too.

Qin Shi Huangdi thought he had founded a dynasty that would last for ten thousand years. But only three years after his death, the Qin Dynasty fell. It was followed by the Han Dynasty, which further united the empire. To this day most people in China refer to themselves as the Han people.

Heading South

At first the center of Chinese civilization was in the northern part of the country, around the Huang He. Sometime about A.D. 1000, however, large numbers of people began to move south. The warmer Chang Jiang region offered a longer growing season and could support more people. Over the centuries southern China outstripped the north in population.

Until the twentieth century, Chinese dynasties rose and tumbled. Under the dynastic system, Chinese society resem-

A warrior in traditional dress stands guard at the Great Wall. When it was finished, sometime during the 1400s, the wall stretched for 1,500 miles (2,400 kilometers) along China's northern border. Today several hundred miles of China's famous defensive wall still stand.

bled an immense pyramid. Millions of peasants formed the pyramid's vast base. At the mercy of droughts, floods, and the emperor's tax collectors, the peasants scraped their living from the land. Above the peasants on the social ladder were the merchants. They sold goods at stalls in local markets, or peddled their wares from village to village. Some traveled the great Silk Road. This famous trade route stretched 4,000 miles (6,436 kilometers) across Asia, from China to Turkey.

Civil servants formed another important level of the social pyramid. At first they came entirely from the upper classes. But by about A.D. 1000, a person could rise in society by

Camel trains like this one once traveled the Silk Road, laden with silks and spices.

passing a civil service test. The tests were extremely difficult and required many years of study. Anyone who passed the exam could get a government job. Thousands of government offices operated all over the empire, staffed by civil servants. It is sometimes said that China gave the world five great inventions: paper, printing, gunpowder, the magnetic compass, and government bureaucracy.

At the top of Chinese society were the courtiers and nobles. At the very peak of the social pyramid reigned the emperor, or Son of Heaven. After A.D. 1421, the emperor and his court occupied the Forbidden City, a walled section of the capital, Beijing (bay-JING). They lived in ornate palaces where armies of servants jumped to their every command. If the nobles were bored, jugglers and dancers appeared to entertain them. If they were tired, musicians lulled them to sleep. A royal chef could get one hundred blows with a stick if the emperor was displeased with his meal.

Zhongghua (joong-gwa), the Chinese people's name for their country, means "central land." The Chinese have always been proud of their civilization and its achievements. For thousands of years they regarded foreigners as barbarians. During the seventeenth and eighteenth centuries, Chinese officials were reluctant to open their seaports to European trading vessels. They had little interest in Western technology. The old ways had served for four thousand years, and they would serve for four thousand more. Only after defeat in a war with Great Britain (1840–1842) and again in a war with Japan (1897) did the Chinese begin to realize that they must enter the modern world.

China Transformed

In 1911 an American-educated Chinese named Sun Yat-sen (soon yaht-SEN) helped overthrow the Qing (ching) Dynasty. For the first time in its history, China attempted to become a republic. Unfortunately the new government quickly broke down. Powerful warlords rose throughout the country, competing for control in a series of civil wars. Then, in 1931, Japan invaded northeastern China. The invasion was a forerunner of the terrible conflict known as World War II. During the war years millions of Chinese soldiers and civilians lost their lives.

At the end of World War II, Japan was defeated. The Chinese republic was under the leadership of Chiang Kai-shek (chang ki-SHECK), who had the support of the United States. But during the 1930s, a powerful new leader had risen in China. He hoped to revolutionize Chinese society under a Communist government, much like that of the Soviet Union to the north. This leader's name was Mao Ze-dong (mow ze-DOONG).

In 1949 Mao Ze-dong drove out Chiang Kai-shek and his followers, the Chinese Nationalists. They went to the island of

Taiwan. Mao Ze-dong renamed his country the People's Republic of China.

Under a Communist system, individuals are not permitted to own private property or to work for personal gain. Instead, everyone is expected to work for the good of the nation as a whole. Communists claim that in this way poverty will disappear and all people can live as equals. The system requires an all-powerful government to enforce its policies.

During the early years under Mao, China made great strides in education, manufacturing, and agriculture. But the country still had a long way to go. In 1958 Mao called for a Great Leap Forward in crop and steel production. Millions of peasants were forced to leave the farms and work in factories. Those who stayed on the land were told to plant the rows of rice close together, so that the fields would resemble "a sky full of stars." The results were disastrous. All over the country, crops failed. Peasants were forced to eat their seed grain and then had nothing to plant the following spring. Mao's Great Leap Forward led to starvation and death for millions of people.

In 1949 Mao Ze-dong led the Communist revolution that transformed Chinese society.

In 1966 Mao launched another experiment that he hoped would strengthen the nation. In order to create a society in which all people would be equal, he decided that every trace of

CHINESE GOVERNMENT

The People's Republic of China is a Communist dictatorship. The Communist Party is the only political party in the nation, controlling all three branches of the government. Although China has a premier, or president, the Communist Party chairman is actually the country's most powerful leader.

The Communist Party selects candidates to run for the National People's Congress, the government's legislative, or lawmaking, branch. On the advice of the Communist Party, the Congress appoints the executive branch—the premier and the State Council. The People's Supreme Court heads China's judicial branch, which interprets the laws. All three branches carry out the policies established by the Communist Party.

the old imperial order had to be swept away. Educated people, such as teachers and doctors, were sent to work like peasants in the fields. Teenagers were urged to challenge anyone who clung to China's old ways. Bands of teens, known as the Red Guard, traveled around the country. They attacked students and teachers and destroyed books, works of art, and even ancient buildings. Thousands of lives were ruined during this chaotic period, which Mao called the Cultural Revolution.

By the mid-1970s, most Chinese people realized that the Cultural Revolution was a terrible mistake. After Mao's death, in 1976, the new leaders worked hard to rebuild the country. China took a fresh interest in the outside world. Gradually, people were allowed to work for some personal profit.

The most heavily populated nation in the world, China faces enormous problems. It remains a Communist nation. At the same time, it is trying to adapt the Communist system to the demands and benefits of free enterprise.

A young "policeman" poses before the Temple of Heaven in Beijing.

2

THE PEOPLE

Standing Room Only

Few families in China can afford an automobile. People go almost everywhere by bicycle and by train. The trains are always packed. People jam together on narrow seats or stand in the aisles with their luggage around them. Travel by train is a good example of the constant crowding that people live with in China.

In area China is only slightly larger than the United States. But with a staggering 1.2 billion people, China has nearly five times the United States population. One out of every five people on earth lives in the People's Republic. City sidewalks are almost impassable because of the throngs of men, women, and children. The Chinese language does not even have a word meaning *privacy*. Living so close together has shaped the way people work and play and the way they view the world around them.

Who Are the Chinese?

More than 90 percent of the people in China consider themselves to be Han Chinese. The Han Chinese live chiefly on the

Above: *Few people in China own cars; children walk to school and adults ride bicycles to work.*

Right: *Pedestrians fight to move along this crowded street in Shanghai.*

eastern plains, especially in the densely populated Chang Jiang delta region. The majority are farmers. More and more people, though, are moving to the cities in search of jobs.

Despite the extraordinary crowding in eastern China, the People's Republic has vast regions with very few people. In some areas of the western mountains, the population averages only one person per square mile (2.6 square kilometers). For the most part the remote western regions are the home of China's minority peoples.

In all, China has more than fifty minority groups. Some, such as the Chuang (ju-AHNG) of the southeast, live much like the Han Chinese. Others have their own distinct languages and customs.

On the sweeping grasslands of Inner Mongolia, nomadic herders tend goats, camels, and cattle. Many Mongolians live in round tents called yurts, moving from place to place as the seasons change. The Dai (die) of Yunnan (yu-NAHN) Province are another minority people who live very differently from the Han Chinese. Most Dai build their homes on stilts, with space underneath to house pigs, chickens, and other livestock. Dai women wear embroidered blouses and colorful turbans.

The Chinese Language

More people speak Chinese than any other language on earth. It is the native tongue of over 1 billion people. The term *Chinese* generally refers to the language that Westerners call Mandarin. Mandarin is the national language of China and is spoken by about 90 percent of the people.

About 100 million of China's citizens do not speak Mandarin. They use any of some fifty other languages, including Cantonese, Fujian, Ammoy, Mongolian, Tibetan, and Dai. Many of the languages spoken by minority peoples in remote areas have no written form.

Westerners often describe Chinese as "a singsong" language. This is because the language is tonal. The meaning of a word depends on the tone in which it is pronounced. Mandarin has four tones: high, high-rising, low-dipping-rising, and high-falling. Its rising and falling tones give Chinese a slightly musical quality that sounds strange to Western ears.

In its written form the English language is based on a phonetic alphabet. Each letter of the alphabet stands for a particular sound. Chinese writing, in contrast, consists of characters, each one a symbol for a specific word or syllable.

Some four thousand years ago, Chinese writing began

with tiny pictures representing objects or events. The ancient symbol for *horse*, for example, was the picture of a galloping steed. Over the centuries, people wanted to write faster, so they made the pictures more and more abstract. Today it is almost impossible to recognize a character simply by its appearance.

Chinese characters must be learned by painstaking memorization. A person needs to know about 2,500 characters to read a newspaper article! For thousands of years, only a few people at the highest levels of Chinese society had the chance to learn to read. Writing—or calligraphy, in which the characters are painted with a brush—developed into an art form for nobles and scholars. It was seldom taught to women. After the Communist Revolution of 1949, the Chinese government began a massive program to bring reading and writing to the common people. Written Mandarin was simplified to make it easier to learn. But learning to read in China still requires a great deal of memorization. Furthermore, characters cannot be written easily with a Western-style typewriter or computer keyboard.

Chinese writing is beautiful and fascinating. But it presents serious problems as China seeks to enter the modern world.

The Life of the Spirit

Until the 1949 revolution, the people of China's upper classes followed one or more of three religious traditions: Confucianism, Daoism, or Buddhism. Each of these religions had a powerful influence on Chinese society. None, however, believed in a deity in any way resembling the Christian God. They can actually best be described as philosophies, or schools of thought.

Today girls as well as boys study the fine arts of calligraphy.

Uneducated peasants borrowed bits and pieces from each of the great Chinese philosophies. Then they wove them into an even older set of beliefs in magic and superstition. Their world was alive with gods and goddesses, ghosts and demons. It is no wonder that a nineteenth-century Christian missionary wrote in frustration, "The educated people believe in nothing, and the uneducated believe in everything!"

The Chinese scholar Kung Fu-zi (kong FOO-zuh), known to Westerners as Confucius, lived during the fifth century B.C. He wandered from court to court, telling the nobles and officials how they should live and govern. Few people paid attention during his lifetime. But in the centuries after his death, Confucius's ideas became very important throughout China.

23

Buddhists celebrate a religious festival before an ancient temple.

Many of his thoughts are captured in brief sayings such as, "What you do not wish for yourself, do not do to others."

Confucius believed that society would run smoothly if each person behaved according to his or her given role. An emperor should be a wise and gentle ruler; a wife should give her husband unwavering support; children should obey their parents and teachers. Confucius wanted an orderly world in which people treated one another fairly and with respect. Strong families were the foundation for a good society.

In many ways Daoism is the direct opposite of Confucianism. Daoism emphasizes the principle of *wu wei* (woo way), or nonaction. Human beings should not push and struggle, but should live in harmony with the natural world.

The third great Chinese philosophy, Buddhism, was started in India in the sixth century B.C. by a prince named Siddhartha (sid-HEARTH-ah) Gautama (GOW-tuh-muh). The prince was raised in great wealth and luxury. Gradually, however, he came to believe that the desire for material things causes much of the suffering in the world. He thought it was better to give up the pursuit of goods and pleasures for a life of the spirit. The prince eventually became known as the Enlightened One, or the Buddha. Through the process of reincarnation, he said, the soul lives a series of lives on earth until it finally reaches perfection. Only then can it achieve its reward, a state of blissful peace. In his teachings the Buddha strongly urged people to behave well toward one another.

Buddhism arrived in China sometime in the first century A.D. and found many followers. Today there are more Buddhists in China than in India. Many of the gods and goddesses known to the Chinese people come from Buddhist myths and legends. Guanyin (gwahn-YEEN) is a merciful goddess who bestows gifts, especially to children. Tudi

Boys begin training at an early age to become Buddhist monks.

Gong (too-DEE goong) is the humble god of hearth and home.

Ancestors have always held a special place in the minds of the Chinese peasants. People fear that the ghosts of their ancestors will cause bad luck if they become angry. To keep their dead grandparents and great-grandparents happy, people prepare rich meals for them at festival times. On some special occasions they burn offerings of paper money as a gift. The people believe that the land of the dead is much like our own world, run by gods who resemble government officials. The dead need money in order to bribe the bureaucrats in the afterlife.

Communism has sometimes been called China's fourth great religion. The Communist Party disapproved of all forms of religious practice. After 1949, traditional beliefs were officially discouraged all over China. Buddhist temples became museums, and religious festivals turned into political holidays. But the ancient beliefs never completely died. When the government relaxed its attitude during the 1980s, the old traditions were ready to resume their place in Chinese life.

A Nation of Farmers

About 75 percent of the Chinese people live in rural areas—in villages of less than 2,500 people. Because of China's immense population, however, even the farmland is crowded with people. As many as thirty villages may be scattered over an area of 20 square miles (52 square kilometers). Each village has about 500 to 1,000 people. The houses, made of sun-dried brick, are built close together and surrounded by fields where crops are planted. The villages have no stores, restaurants, or other businesses. To shop, people travel to the nearest market town. There farm families can buy and sell produce and can purchase the few manufactured goods that are available.

With its long, harsh winters, northern China has a fairly short growing season. In southern China, on the other hand, work on the farms continues almost year-round. In the Chang Jiang delta region, the landscape is composed almost entirely of irrigated rice paddies. The paddies are separated by earthen dikes that also serve as walkways and paths for wheelbarrows. Oxen and water buffalo are still widely used for plowing. Delta villages are linked by a sprawling network of streams and

A duck herder tends his flock on a river in southern China.

man-made canals. People often travel by boat to visit their friends and relatives.

Because farmland is so scarce, the Chinese make use of every inch of tillable soil. Over the centuries they have carved steplike terraces into the hillsides, creating level fields where crops can grow. In the hilly regions of southeastern China, these terraces are used especially for the growing of tea. Certain gardens are famous for particular teas, which are prized throughout the world.

Communism brought massive changes to the way in which farming was done in China. Instead of tilling family-owned fields, the peasants were ordered to work on large farming communes. A commune might have as many as 100,000 members, drawing on the people from twenty villages or more.

For thousands of years, the peasants had worked their own land. They did not adjust easily to the new system. Few communes were as productive as the government had hoped they would be. In the late 1970s, the government began to dissolve the communes and return the people to family-run farms.

Industrial China

A Chinese man or woman who holds a job in a state-run factory is said to "chew grain." To lose one's job is to "break the rice bowl." These expressions show that a job in a state-run factory offers an enviable sense of security. A worker can not only count on a steady salary, but housing, health care, and an education as well. If a worker becomes ill or disabled, he or she will be taken care of for life.

Most factories are located in eastern cities such as Beijing and Shanghai. But the Chinese government has also encouraged industry to develop in the thinly populated western regions.

As in agriculture, the Chinese are beginning to permit private ownership and individual profit in industry. But as the system changes, workers lose many of the benefits they counted on when they could "chew grain."

Many Chinese factory workers live in small, modest homes like these.

An enormous model of a dragon highlights a New Year's festival in Hong Kong.

3

FAMILY LIFE, FESTIVALS, AND FOOD

The Chinese Way, Then and Now

Every afternoon at one o'clock, the people of China take a nap. Schoolchildren put their heads down on their desks. Busy homemakers draw the shades and stretch out on a couch. Even bankers close their eyes and nod in their chairs. Foreigners doing business in China are amazed by this custom. How, they demand, can the Chinese get anything done? But the Chinese firmly believe that an afternoon rest is essential for good health. The one o'clock nap is a time-honored practice that shows no sign of disappearing.

Some ancient customs in China have disappeared, though. Since the 1949 revolution, China has undergone staggering changes. Communism transformed family life and reshaped the ways in which people dress, cook, and celebrate holidays. Today China is an extraordinary blend of ancient traditions and modern ways.

Men, Women, and Children

In some parts of China, a bride-to-be heaps curses on her future mother-in-law for three days before the wedding. This custom is hardly surprising, considering what married women have endured at the hands of their husbands' mothers for thousands of years.

GOLDEN LOTUSES

For more than a thousand years, standards of beauty required girls in northern China to have extremely tiny feet. When a girl was seven years old, her toes were forcibly curled under, and her feet were wrapped in tight bandages to hold them in this position. Every few weeks the bandages were wound even tighter. The bones of her feet were broken and made to grow twisted and stunted. This agonizing process of foot binding continued for ten years, until the girl finished growing. As a woman, she had to take small, dainty steps on feet that were only 3 inches (7.6 centimeters) long. Her tortured feet, which never completely healed, caused her a lifetime of pain.

A woman whose feet were never bound was considered ugly and undesirable. Tiny bound feet were referred to as "golden lotuses." Foot binding was outlawed in 1911, but for decades afterward Chinese women still hobbled about on feet that had been bound when they were young.

Until 1949, most marriages were arranged by the parents of the bride and groom, usually with the help of a matchmaker. The couple had no chance to become acquainted, or even to meet, before the wedding. When she married, a woman left her parents' home forever and moved in with her husband's family. In the groom's household she was often treated like a slave, without rights or privileges. Her mother-in-law demanded total obedience and was rarely satisfied with the way her daughter-in-law cooked, mended, or swept the floor. Above all, the bride was expected to give birth to children—to sons and heirs.

"How sad it is to be a woman!" lamented a third-century

poet. "Nothing on earth is held so cheap." The birth of a girl triggered tears of grief and shame. Because a girl would grow up and belong to her husband's family, daughters were regarded as worthless burdens. The birth of a son, however, was cause for joyful celebration.

Sons were vital in a traditional Chinese family. It was their duty to operate the family farm or business. Even more important, they were expected to care for their aging parents and to honor the family's ancestors at ceremonies and festivals.

According to Confucius, children must respect and obey their parents at all times. This respect for parental authority extended back through the generations, past the grandparents to long-dead great-grandparents, great-great-grandparents, and beyond. If they did not receive proper honors, the spirits of these ancestors could punish a family by sending them bad

At a traditional wedding, a bridal party poses for a portrait.

According to tradition, elderly people in China are given special respect.

luck. If they were treated with respect, they could keep the family healthy and prosperous. Daughters could not perform the ceremonies necessary to make the ancestors happy. That duty rested on the shoulders of the sons alone.

The Family Revised

The Communist Revolution attempted to create a society in which everyone would be treated equally. The government tried to eliminate inequalities between men and women and between the wealthy and the poor. As new schools opened their doors, girls were expected to study along with their brothers. New laws abolished arranged marriages. For the first time in China's long history, young people were free to choose their own marriage partners.

The government has worked hard to convince the Chinese people that girls are as valuable as boys. Yet the beliefs of thousands of years do not change overnight. For both women and men, life in China has often been cruelly hard. But at festival time, troubles are forgotten and everyone has fun.

Renao: **Noise and Commotion**

Many Chinese words have no direct translation in English. One such word is *renao* (reh-NOW). Roughly it means "noisy and boisterous, lively and exciting." The word *renao* is a good description of a Chinese festival.

The most important holiday in China is Xin Nian (SHEEN nee-EN), or Chinese New Year. China officially follows the Western calendar, beginning the year on January 1. But the Chinese people still celebrate the new year according to the ancient lunar calendar, which varies from year to year according to the phases of the moon. The new year begins with the new moon, anywhere between January 21 and February 19. The festival lasts for about two weeks.

During the new year festival, the troubles of the old year are swept away. People prepare for a lucky and prosperous future. No negative words may be uttered. Only cheerful thoughts may be spoken aloud. For days each household hosts a series of dinner parties, attended by relatives who have traveled home for this special occasion. The foods served at these meals all have symbolic meaning. For example, kumquats (small citrus fruits) stand for prosperity, because the Chinese character for *kumquats* also means "gold."

The new year is also celebrated with music, dance, and processions. In many parts of China, a splendid Xin Nian parade is headed by lion dancers. Two or more men hide inside an enormous papier-mâché lion. The lion crouches, leaps, and stretches magnificently. It is followed by colorfully dressed clowns, acrobats, and musicians. Fireworks displays are a favorite part of the new year celebration. On streets and in public squares, crowds gather to enjoy the din and blaze of colored rockets and sparkling pinwheels.

At festival time, some women wear dazzling costumes.

After two weeks the new year festivities come to a close with the Lantern Festival. Houses, shops, and even government buildings are adorned with a dazzling array of colored lanterns. Some are made of paper, some of glass, some even of silk. Shaped like birds, dragonflies, and fish, like the sun, the moon, and the stars, the lanterns give the new year a glorious welcome.

Xin Nian is a festival of renewal; Qingming Jie (ching-ming gee-EH) is a feast to honor the dead. Qingming, or the Feast of Pure Brightness, is held on April 4, 5, or 6. Families prepare special meals for their deceased relatives. After the

Representing strength and fertility, the dragon is an important symbol during the Festival of the New Year.

ghosts of the departed have a chance to enjoy the essence of the delicious food, the living sit down to devour the meal.

During Qingming, people visit their ancestors' graves. They pull weeds, sweep dirt from the tombs, and leave offerings of food for the dead. This attention keeps the ancestors happy and insures that they will bring good fortune. After the graves have been properly tended, the mood shifts. The graveyard becomes a scene of festivity, with picnics and kite flying.

One of the most unusual Chinese holidays is the Dragon Boat Festival, celebrated each year around June 21. All over southern China, crowds gather to watch races between long, slender rowboats. The boats are painted in bright colors and decorated to resemble dragons. Each has a carved dragon's head at the bow and a scaly, twisting tail at the stern. The dragon is a symbol of strength and fertility, and this festival is connected with the growth of summer crops.

The Mid-Autumn Feast, or Zhongqiu Jie (joong-chee-oh gee-EH), is a quiet time of reunion and thanksgiving. It occurs in mid-September, when the rice or wheat has been harvested and the moon is brighter than at any other time of the year. For Zhongqiu, people gather in parks and gardens to drink tea, eat fresh fruit, and gaze at the moon. The moon's roundness is a symbol of unity and harmony. Round pastries called mooncakes are among this holiday's treats. Mooncakes are filled with sweet red-bean or lotus-seed paste, or sometimes with a mixture of ground nuts, raisins, and coconut.

Qingming, Zhongqiu, and many other festivals date back thousands of years. But China has added some new holidays since the Communist Revolution. Like most Communist countries, it honors working men and women on International Workers' Day, May 1. All workers have the day off to enjoy picnics, dancing, and fireworks. National Day (October 1) commemorates Mao Ze-dong's triumphant march into Beijing in 1949. Schoolchildren and workers march in parades and listen to speeches at mass rallies.

When Chinese children look forward to Xin Nian, Zhongqiu, or any other festival, they talk about steamed dumplings, spicy pork and chicken, and tempting mooncakes. Food is an essential part of every holiday. In a country that has known more than its share of famines, food takes on special meaning and importance.

Glorious Food

To many Americans, Chinese food means chop suey and egg rolls from a take-out counter. These favorites evolved from dishes that were popular in and around the city of Guangzhou (gwahng-CHOH), formerly called Canton. But the Cantonese food served in most United States restaurants has little in common with real Chinese food, the food people eat in China.

In southern China, rice is the basic ingredient of nearly every meal. In the north, where the main crop is wheat, many dishes use thin wheat noodles resembling Italian pasta. Chinese cooking has many other regional differences as well. The Province of Sichuan (si-CHWAHN) is noted for dishes made with fiery hot peppers. Seafood is plentiful in the southeast, around the Chang Jiang delta, and crabmeat is that region's delicacy.

A mother instructs her child in the proper use of chopsticks.

Since China has few forests, Chinese cooks have never had much firewood for fuel. They learned to cook a full meal with only a few fast-burning twigs. This method of quick cooking is called stir frying. Meat and vegetables are carefully

STIR-FRIED ZUCCHINI WITH GARLIC

Most Chinese dishes are stir-fried in oil over a very high flame. Get an adult to help you when you follow this recipe.

1 pound zucchini   *2 cloves garlic, finely sliced*
1+ teaspoons salt   *1 teaspoon sugar*
3 tablespoons oil

Grate the zucchini into a colander with a vegetable grater. Sprinkle with salt and stir thoroughly. Let the mixture stand for 15 minutes. With your hands, gently squeeze out any excess moisture. Salting the zucchini in this way lessens the bitter taste of the skin.

Heat the oil in a wok and add the finely sliced garlic. Stir for 20 seconds. Add the zucchini and sugar, and stir for 2 more minutes. Remove from the heat and serve. Serves 2–3.

cut into little pieces. Then they are cooked on a fast, high flame in a small amount of oil. The wok, an iron pan with rounded bottom and sides, allows food to cook rapidly and evenly.

At holiday time, people feast on foods that are unknown during the rest of the year. On ordinary days, Chinese meals are quite simple. A typical midday meal in south China consists of steamed rice and stir-fried vegetables, followed by a bowl of vegetable soup. In China, soup is always served at the end of a meal. Desserts are rare; if you go to China, don't expect to be handed a fortune cookie!

Whatever the meal, it is never eaten with a knife and fork. All the cutting is done in the kitchen before serving. Food comes to the table in bite-sized pieces that can easily be grasped between a pair of chopsticks. For Westerners, this method can be a struggle at first. But once mastered, eating with chopsticks is easy and graceful.

Whether a meal is a holiday banquet or a humble bowl of rice, food is central to social life in China. It is no wonder that the standard greeting between friends is not, "How are you?" but rather, "Have you eaten?"

Dressing Down and Dressing Up

In the first decades after the Communist Revolution, fancy dress was strictly forbidden. Men and women wore simple cotton pants and shirts of black, blue, or gray. Today, however, the Chinese enjoy fashion more. In the cities people wear Western-style clothes bought in stores. The styles are similar in the country, though the clothing is usually homemade.

Since the early 1980s the Chinese government has encouraged people of ethnic minorities to wear their traditional costumes. Traditional

A Miao woman in traditional dress

apparel is usually seen in rural areas, or in towns and cities during festivals. The Miao (mee-OW) of Guizhou (gwee-CHOH) Province are among the minorities famous for their elaborate dress. Miao women wear brightly colored, embroidered clothes, laden with jewelry. As they walk, they jingle with silver necklaces and bracelets.

41

A preschooler experiments with paints.

4

SCHOOL AND RECREATION

Time for Study, Time for Play

Every evening in towns and cities across China, thousands of men and women pore over books in crowded classrooms. They have worked all day, but they are not ready to go home yet. They are studying in night school, striving to advance their educations.

Many of these night-school students grew up during the Cultural Revolution of 1966–1976. Throughout that turbulent decade, study was frowned upon as old-fashioned and snobbish. Students criticized and even attacked their teachers, and most schools closed. But respect for learning is an ancient tradition in China. After the Cultural Revolution, the government once more launched its campaign to educate the nation's vast population. The "lost generation" of the Cultural Revolution struggles for the knowledge it was once denied.

Going to School

Small children in China are seldom scolded or punished. Until the youngsters reach the age of five or six, their parents and older siblings shower them with attention. Perhaps children are indulged when they are little because their elders feel sorry for them. They know what lies ahead for them when they enter school.

Children start school when they are six years old, and from that time forward they must be well behaved and responsible, like little adults. At school they have to sit quietly, obey the teacher, and study very hard. Reading and writing in Chinese call for intensive memorization. By the end of first grade, a child is expected to master at least six hundred characters. Children who speak Cantonese, Fujian, or Tibetan as their first language must also begin learning Mandarin.

Students remain in primary school until age twelve. At that point they move on to lower middle school, which they attend until they are sixteen. Many students drop out of lower middle school to work in the fields or factories. Those who

Students work with the abacus, a traditional method for doing arithmetic.

Many students learn to play musical instruments after school.

continue their studies move on to upper middle school, remaining to age eighteen.

In order to enter a university, an upper-middle-school graduate must pass a series of very difficult examinations. Students are under tremendous pressure to study for these exams. Yet only about one in ten manages to pass.

The school day for primary pupils begins early, at seven-thirty in the morning. About half of the school day is devoted to reading and writing Chinese characters. Students also study science, social studies, physical education, and mathematics, which uses the same number system used in the United States. The children have a chance to relax during the ten-minute recesses between classes. After lunch there is an hour-long rest period for students and teachers alike. The school day ends at three-thirty in the afternoon.

American children are often encouraged to compete with one another, to stand up for their rights. In China, where people live at very close quarters, children are taught to be cooperative. Children learn too that each person has a role in improving society for everyone. To encourage youngsters to be helpful, most teachers post lists of good deeds that their students have done at home and at school. At the end of the year, the school makes a special announcement of the total number of good deeds its pupils have performed.

Playing After Hours

Chinese children usually have about three hours of homework every night. But between three-thirty and five they have time to enjoy themselves. On playgrounds and sidewalks, girls jump rope and play a game similar to American hopscotch. Older boys spin special wooden tops. Struck with a kind of lash or whip, these tops spin with astonishing speed.

In addition to sidewalk games, most children participate in some form of organized athletics. Many Western games are popular in China. Most schools have basketball, soccer, and volleyball teams. Ping-Pong has been a favorite since the 1950s. Both boys and girls take part in gymnastics, training for competitions between schools or villages.

Physical exercise is a vital part of every school day.

Adults, too, have time for recreation after their workday is over. Most communes sponsor basketball and soccer teams. People also enjoy swimming, ice-skating, and roller-skating.

Adults frequently play quieter games, such as mahjongg (mah-JONG) and chess. In mahjongg, a game of strategy and chance, four players use thick ivory or wooden tiles. Most of the fun comes from betting on the outcome. Chess is often played in public parks and tea shops. Huge crowds gather to watch outdoor chess tournaments in Guangzhou's Cultural Park. There, a spotlight shines on a gigantic board and each move is announced over a public-address system.

Strolling in the Park

The emperor Kublai Khan once created a splendid park in Beijing. Every species of tree known in all of China was planted there. For thousands of years, such parks could be enjoyed

47

only by nobles and government officials. Since 1949, however, China's parks have been open to everyone. On warm evenings and summer weekends, they overflow with families who have come to relax and have fun.

One of the most popular activities in the parks is kite flying. Kites have been used in China since ancient times. Over the years they have become an art form. Some resemble birds, fish, or airplanes. Some make whistling or clicking sounds as they soar through the sky. Some kites measure up to 15 feet (4.6 meters) in length, and tug so hard in the wind that several people must clutch the string.

Since ancient times, the Chinese have flown kites of all shapes.

Many people bring live birds in cages to the parks. The Chinese love songbirds and keep many kinds as pets. In the parks they show off their favorites and give the birds a taste of fresh air.

Whether in a small town or in a great city like Beijing, the parks are a magnet for musicians, dancers, storytellers, jugglers, and acrobats. Many of these entertainers travel from town to town in organized troupes sponsored by the government. Probably the most remarkable of these performers are the stilt walkers. They tower above the spectators on stilts 12 feet (3.7 meters) tall. As they prance about, they look like enormous grasshoppers. How did they learn to keep their balance? Like so many other arts in China, stilt walking simply calls for years of patient practice.

Stilt walkers perform in a Chinese park.

In Beijing the opera is a celebration in costume, dance, and song.

5

THE ARTS

Things of Beauty

The emperor Qin Shi Huangdi, who united the land we know as China, was buried in a magnificent tomb near the city of Xian (shee-AHN). Across its floor sprawled a map of his domain. The ceiling was painted with a view of the heavens, showing all the known planets and stars. The tomb was staffed with an army of about six thousand soldiers—each carefully shaped of a clay called terra-cotta. The soldiers were life-size, and no two were alike. Some marched, some prepared food, some stood sentry duty. Each was an individual, his face and pose unique.

Thousands of master sculptors must have worked to create this terra-cotta army, which was unearthed by archaeologists in 1974. It is a stunning example of the creative achievements of China's artists, achievements that can be traced back to the dawn of the nation's history.

Light as Brush Strokes, Heavy as Stone

In a huge cave northwest of the city of Chong Qing, the ancient legends of the Buddhists spring to life. The walls of the cave are carved with thousands of animal and human figures, all enacting famous episodes from age-old Buddhist stories. These sculptures at Bao Ding Shan (bow ding SHAHN), "Many-Peaked Mountain," are typical of Buddhist art found all over China.

Pottery has long been a way for artists to express themselves in China. Vases, cups, lamps, and other objects were given beautifully balanced forms and painted with flowers, birds, and animals. The exquisite porcelains created during the Yuan (1279–1362) and Ming dynasties (1368–1644) are almost priceless today.

Drawing in China is a natural outgrowth of calligraphy, or Chinese character writing. During the Tang Dynasty

The terra-cotta army of Xian is one of the most spectacular discoveries in modern times.

(618–907), painters created landscapes in a single, flowing stroke, never lifting the brush from the paper. Later painting used more realistic detail. For centuries nature was the favorite theme of Chinese painters. But in the twentieth century, artists used their work to convey political messages. Many pictures showed the hardships of peasant life before the revolution and the accomplishments of people working together under communism.

In the days of imperial China, the wealthy nobles enjoyed designing their own miniature worlds in the form of landscaped gardens. Stone bridges arched over ponds alive with goldfish. Fountains tumbled down terraced hillsides. Paths meandered among trees and beds of flowers. Here and there stood a gazebo, or roofed shelter, where the stroller could pause to rest. Often a poem was inscribed above the doorway, putting the beauty and purity of nature into words.

"NIGHT IN THE PAVILION BY THE RIVER"

Evening haze creeps up hill paths,
I lie in the pavilion overlooking
The river; light clouds envelop
Cliff sides, and the moon's reflection
Is twisted by the waters;
Cranes and storks rest after
Their flight; wild beasts howl
As they seek their prey; sleep
Does not come to me, for still
I worry about war, knowing I have
No way to set the world aright.

—Du Fu (A.D. 712–770)

The Love of Language

Until the eighteenth century, at least half of all the books on earth were written in Chinese. Like so much else in China, the literary tradition stretches back to ancient times. The earliest

The grace and beauty of birds have inspired many Chinese paintings.

known writings were inscriptions on bones and pieces of tortoiseshell, dating back to about 1400 B.C. These bones were used for telling fortunes. Among the first actual books were a collection of sayings by the philosopher Confucius.

During the Tang Dynasty, poetry flourished in China. The two most famous poets of this era are Du Fu and Li Po. Du Fu wrote about the pleasures and responsibilities of family life. Sometimes he described the injustices he saw in society. Li Po, on the other hand, was a happy-go-lucky person who wrote about love, friendship, and wine. According to legend, he drowned when he fell out of a boat as he tried to embrace the moon's reflection in the water. One famous work of this period is *The Ballad of Mulan* by the woman poet Zu Yeh. It recounts the adventures of a woman who disguises herself as a man and becomes a soldier.

Fiction appeared in China several centuries before it developed in the West. China's two great novels were written in the fourteenth century. *The Romance of the Three Kingdoms* is a long story about warfare, and *The Water Margin* deals with bandits and heroes.

As is true with painting, much twentieth-century literature carries a strong message about the social inequalities that finally led to the Communist Revolution. In the 1970s and 1980s, however, writers began to explore new subjects and described the everyday lives of ordinary people.

At one time only the wealthy could enjoy landscaped gardens; today they are open to everyone.

Singing of Forests

According to Confucius, music was not meant to entertain its listeners but to calm and purify the spirit. This belief survived through the ages and is still held by some Chinese musicians today. The *qin* (chin) is an ancient stringed instrument resembling the Western zither. It is prized for its calming virtues. One long-ago scholar wrote, "Though the *qin* player's body be in a gallery or in a hall, his mind should dwell with the forests and streams."

In Guizhou Province, Miao musicians play bamboo flutes and other traditional instruments.

Because scholars and nobles frowned on music played for mere entertainment, many musicians were looked down on until modern times. Yet music was always an important part of every Chinese festival, and singers and flute players often performed on the streets. Today the Chinese government has given popular music a new respect as one of the people's art forms.

Another kind of music is enjoyed all over China—the opera. Most Americans think of an evening at the opera as a serious, formal event. In China, however, the opera is a festive occasion, thoroughly enjoyed by young and old. People drink tea, munch snacks, and cheer whenever their favorite characters appear.

For hundreds of years Chinese operas were based on ancient tales of warriors, gods, and demons. Today's performances celebrate the heroic deeds of Communist revolutionaries. But the old stories also remain popular. The opera has changed very little over the centuries. It is still a glorious spectacle of elaborate costume, song, and graceful, dancelike movements. It is a time for people to step away from their lives of work and study and to enjoy being together. It is a time for people to feel themselves once again part of the endless tradition that is the land of China.

Country Facts

Official Name: Zhongghua Renmin Gongheguo (People's Republic of China)

Capital: Beijing

Location: in the eastern part of Asia, bordered on the north by Russia (former Soviet Union), Outer Mongolia, and North Korea; on the east and southeast by the Pacific Ocean; on the south by Vietnam, Laos, Myanmar (Burma), India, Bhutan, and Nepal; and on the west by Pakistan and Afghanistan

Area: 3,696,032 square miles (9,572,723) kilometers. *Greatest distances:* east–west, 3,000 miles (4,827 kilometers); north–south, 2,500 miles (4,023 kilometers). *Coastline:* 4,019 miles (6,467 kilometers)

Elevation: *Highest:* Mount Everest, in the Himalayas, 29,028 feet (8,848 meters). *Lowest:* Turfan Depression, near the northern edge of Takla Makan Desert, 505 feet (154 meters) below sea level

Climate: ranges from long, cold winters in northern and western areas, to mild and warm in central and southern China. Summers are hot and humid in eastern half and hot and dry in northwestern deserts.

Population: 1,238,319,000. *Distribution:* 26 percent urban; 74 percent rural

Form of Government: Communist dictatorship

Important Products: *Agriculture:* rice, wheat, corn, soybeans, tea, cotton, tobacco, fruit, potatoes. *Industries:* textiles, steelmaking, food processing, tourism, plastics, mining, shipbuilding. *Natural Resources:* coal, petroleum, iron ore, tungsten

Basic Unit of Money: yuan; 1 yuan = 100 fen

Language: Mandarin Chinese is official language; other languages include Cantonese, Ammoy, Fujian, Tibetan, and Mongolian.

Religion: traditionally: Confucianism, Daoism, and Buddhism; small Christian and Islamic minorities

Flag: one large yellow star, four small yellow stars in upper left corner, on red background

National Anthem: *Yiyongjun Jinxingqu* (YEE-yoong-joon CHIN-shing-choo), "March of the Volunteers"

Major Holidays: New Year's Day, January 1; Chinese New Year, depending on phases of moon, celebrated between January and February; Feast of Pure Brightness, April 4, 5, or 6; International Workers' Day, May 1; Children's Day, June 1; Mid-Autumn Feast, mid-September; National Day, October 1

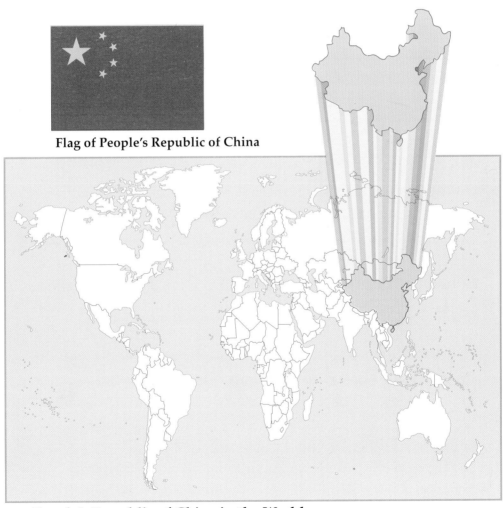

Flag of People's Republic of China

People's Republic of China in the World

Glossary

archaeologist: a person who studies the way humans lived long ago. Archaeologists dig up the remains of ancient cities and then study the tools, pottery, weapons, and other objects they find.

Buddhism: a religion that came to China from India. Buddhists believe that the soul comes to earth repeatedly, in many forms, until it achieves a state of perfect purity.

bureaucracy: a complex system of running a government based on various bureaus and departments, each with a separate set of responsibilities. The people who work in these government offices are called **bureaucrats**.

calligraphy: the writing of Chinese characters as a form of decorative art

communism: a political system based on the idea that all economic profit should go to the state. The state will then distribute money and goods to the people as they are needed.

Confucianism: a Chinese philosophy. It encourages people to be truthful and virtuous.

Daoism: a Chinese philosophy. It emphasizes the place of humans in the natural world and the need for balance and harmony.

delta: rich, fertile land near the mouth of a river

dynasty: a series of rulers who belong to the same family. One dynasty may rule for hundreds of years.

free enterprise: an economic system based on personal profit for the individual

levee: a barricade of earth and sandbags used to keep a river from overflowing

mandate: order or command

nomadic: having to do with nomads or with wandering from place to place

peasant: farm laborer of the lowest social class

plateau: area of flat land that is raised above the surrounding country

reincarnation: the belief that after a person dies, the soul is re-born in another body, which may be human or animal

republic: form of government in which the authority belongs to the people. The people elect representatives to run the government.

stir fry: a method of cooking used in China, in which food is chopped fine and cooked quickly in oil over a high flame

wok: a pan, with rounded bottom and sides, that allows for quick, even cooking

wu wei (woo way)*:* the basic principle of Daoism, the idea of natural flow or harmony

For Further Reading

Brooke, William J. *A Brush with Magic*. New York: Harper-Collins, 1993 (fiction).

Carter, Alden R. *China Past—China Future*. New York: Franklin Watts, 1994.

Chrisman, Arthur Bowie. *Shen of the Sea*. New York: E. P. Dutton, 1967.

Fisher, Leonard Everett. *The Great Wall of China*. New York: Macmillan, 1986.

Kendall, Carol. *Sweet and Sour: Tales from China*. Boston: Clarion, 1990.

Lewis, Elizabeth F. *Young Fu of the Upper Yangtze*. New York: Dell, 1990 (fiction).

Li Shufen, ed. *Legends of Ten Chinese Traditional Festivals*. San Francisco: China Books, 1992.

Mahy, Margaret. *Seven Chinese Brothers*. New York: Scholastic, 1990 (fiction).

Major, John S. *The Silk Route*. New York: HarperCollins, 1994.

Marrin, Albert. *Mao Tse-Tung and His China*. New York: Puffin, 1993.

Patterson, Katherine. *Rebels of the Heavenly Kingdom*. New York: Dutton, 1983 (fiction).

Rau, Margaret. *Young Women in China*. Hillside, New Jersey: Enslow, 1989.

Shui, Amy, and Stuart Thompson. *Chinese Food and Drink*. New York: Bookwright Press, 1987.

Teague, Ken. *Growing up in Ancient China*. Mahwah, New Jersey: Troll, 1993.

Thompson, Peggy. *City Kids in China*. New York: HarperCollins, 1991.

Index

About the Author

Deborah Kent grew up in Little Falls, New Jersey, and received her B.A. degree from Oberlin College. Before launching her writing career, she did social work in New York City and helped start a school for disabled children in San Miguel de Allende, Mexico. Ms. Kent has written more than a dozen young-adult novels, as well as numerous nonfiction books for children. She lives in Chicago with her husband, children's book author R. Conrad Stein, and their daughter, Janna.